EASY AS ABC

Cc

Warren Rylands and Aaron Carr

www.av2books.com

AV² provides enriched content that supplements and complements this book. Weigl's AV² books strive to create inspired learning and engage young minds in a total learning experience.

Your AV² Media Enhanced books come alive with...

Audio
Listen to sections of the book read aloud.

Video
Watch informative video clips.

Embedded Weblinks
Gain additional information for research.

Try This!
Complete activities and hands-on experiments.

Key Words
Study vocabulary, and complete a matching word activity.

Quizzes
Test your knowledge.

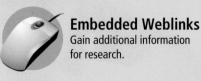
Slide Show
View images and captions, and prepare a presentation.

... and much, much more!

Go to **www.av2books.com**, and enter this book's unique code.

BOOK CODE

E963992

AV² by Weigl brings you media enhanced books that support active learning.

Published by AV² by Weigl
350 5ᵗʰ Avenue, 59ᵗʰ Floor
New York, NY 10118

Website: www.av2books.com

Copyright ©2016 AV² by Weigl

Library of Congress Control Number: 2015940605

ISBN 978-1-4896-3475-7 (hardcover)
ISBN 978-1-4896-3477-1 (single user eBook)
ISBN 978-1-4896-3478-8 (multi-user eBook)

Printed in the United States of America in Brainerd, Minnesota
1 2 3 4 5 6 7 8 9 0 19 18 17 16 15

052015
WEP050815

Project Coordinator: Katie Gillespie   Art Director: Terry Paulhus

Weigl acknowledges Getty Images and iStock as the primary image suppliers for this title.

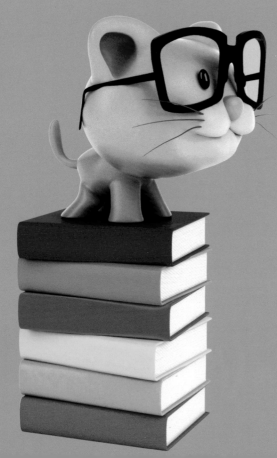

CONTENTS

Let's explore the letter

The uppercase letter C looks like this

The lowercase letter C looks like this

The letter C can start many words.

cow

cowboy

cake

cookie

camel

7

The letter C can be inside a word.

mice

cricket

ice

bacon

tractor

9

The letter c can be

at the end of a word.

tropi

music

arctic

picnic

magic

Many names start with an uppercase C.

Cindy

Carl likes to read.

Cheryl loves flowers.

Chris loves healthy food.

Charles is loud.

13

The letter C makes different sounds.

cat

cereal

The word **cat**
has a hard c sound.

 The word **cereal**
has a soft c sound.

Some words have
a hard C sound.
A hard c sounds
like a k.

cake

card

carrot

cold

cup

17

Other words have
a soft C sound.
A soft c sounds
like an s.

18

cell

cent

pencil

face

juice

19

Having Fun with C

Cheryl put crispy bacon in her cereal. All the cool cowgirls eat cold bacon!

Cheryl could not wait for the cool cowboy picnic.

Chris brought cranberry juice. Charles came with a cup of carrots.

They rode the magic tractor until five o'clock. Then, it was time for cookies and cake!

The alphabet
has 26 letters.

C is the third letter
in the alphabet.

Aa Bb Cc Dd Ee

Ff Gg Hh Ii Jj Kk

Ll Mm Nn Oo Pp

Qq Rr Ss Tt Uu Vv

Ww Xx Yy Zz

23